Lowering Cholesterol

50 Simple Ways to Get Your Cholesterol Down Naturally and Dramatically Improve Your Health

Lisa Lee

Lowering Cholesterol

Copyright © 2012 by Lisa Lee

Disclaimer and Terms of Use: The Author and Publisher has strived to be as accurate and complete as possible in the creation of this book, notwithstanding the fact that he does not warrant or represent at any time that the contents within are accurate due to the rapidly changing nature of the Internet. While all attempts have been made to verify information provided in this publication, the Author and Publisher assumes no responsibility for errors, omissions, or contrary interpretation of the subject matter herein. Any perceived slights of specific persons, peoples, or organizations are unintentional. In practical advice books, like anything else in life, there are no guarantees of income made. This book is not intended for use as a source of legal, business, accounting or financial advice. All readers are advised to seek services of competent professionals in legal, business, medical, accounting, and finance field.

ISBN-13: 978-1470174187
ISBN-10: 1470174189

About The Author

Perhaps one of the most divisive voices in the health world, Lisa Lee is the host of her own nationally syndicated radio show, where she is known for her shoot from the hip attitude that aims to wake people up from their overly processed food comas and start taking control of their own health. Touted by the likes of Morgan Spurlock, and demonized by the shareholders of KFC, Lee's battle-cry "Eat Fast Food, You're Totally screwed," boils down her message and takes her fight directly to those she views as responsible for the clogging of our nation's arteries.

Though her place in the cultural zeitgeist has been fairly solidified for the past decade or so, Lee had never planned on taking on the role of a public advocate. Lee had planned on a career as a general practitioner, expecting to spend her days treating families in some small town practice. In her autobiography, Lee states that the death of her father from a severe heart attack drove her to realize that people truly weren't aware of the damage a bad diet could do to their bodies.

Starting out with a modest approach of writing letters to the editor to her local paper, she soon began receiving letters of her own from fans who appreciated her lack of sugar coating, and some of those letters were offers for work as a columnist and speaker at health events. Almost two years to the date of her father's passing, Lee found herself so busy traveling the country for speaking engagements, television appearances, and hard at work on her first book, when she was forced to temporarily pause her ambitions for becoming a local GP and focus on her new role, as the "defiant voice of the bodies we seem intent on destroying."

The book, named after her famous battle-cry, became an Amazon Bestseller, and was followed by Devil's Food: The Hidden Evils In Your Shopping Cart, and Lisa's Gamechangers, a guide to home-made and healthier versions of popular restaurant fare, and of course her popular radio show. Though she occasionally falls under criticism for her sometimes harsh way of speaking, Lee embraces her image in pop culture, even going so far as to appear in a Saturday Night Live sketch that lampooned herself, as portrayed by Kirsten Wig.

Recently, Lee signed a deal to executive produce and star in Food For Life a new travel series that she touts as "Man Versus Food for those who don't want to kill themselves," where she will travel the country in search of the healthiest and tastiest meals in America. She also is reportedly in talks to launch her own frozen health food line.

Lee still lives in Columbus, OH, where she tapes her syndicated show. When she manages to find some free time, she enjoys cooking and exercising with her loving husband of 25 years, and her two teenage children, who she claims are the hardest two people to convince to put down the fast food.

Connect With Lisa!

facebook.com/LisaLeesPage

Table of Contents

Introduction

This book is an introduction to the 50 most important remedies for lowering cholesterol naturally, which include food, dietary supplements and behavioural methods. We believe that these cholesterol remedies will effectively lower the 'bad' LDL cholesterol, significantly elevate the 'good' HDL cholesterol or reduce the amount of triglycerides (neutral lipids).

Since the World War II, the most common cause of death in the Western world is due to cardio-vascular disease and the most important risk factors are: being overweight and obesity, lack of exercise, Diabetes mellitus (especially Type 2 Diabetes), smoking, hereditary factors, overeating, poor diet, and last but not least, high blood lipid values.

Up to 75% of adults in industrialised countries suffer from increased cholesterol levels of more than 200 mg/dL. Every year hundreds of millions of dollars are spent on cholesterol and lipid lowering drugs by health insurance companies. Patients and doctors alike are seeking alternative treatments for high blood lipid values, mostly because of the worrying safety issues raised in relation to this drug group.

For two thirds of all people suffering from high blood lipid values, the need to take medicines could simply be eliminated by a simple change in diet or lifestyle. If, after several weeks or months, a change in diet and the use of natural cholesterol fighting substances does not have the desired effect of reducing your LDL cholesterol values, it is sensible and necessary to begin taking the usual medication.

What is Cholesterol?

Cholesterol is an essential lipid that exists in all human and animal cells. It is a necessary building block of cell walls and serves as a basis for steroid hormones and bile acids. Plants and seeds contain so-called phytosterols that are similar to cholesterol, but any diet based on plants is guaranteed to be cholesterol-free.

The bulk of cholesterol is manufactured by the body; only a small amount is added via food intake, and of that only 40-50% is utilised in the body. Therefore, we should not focus on the amount of cholesterol we consume, but the quality of the food we eat.

Minimising your cholesterol intake actually leads to an increase in the body's own production of cholesterol, whereas a high intake reduces the amount that the body produces. Avoiding cholesterol altogether is not recommended, however, you should not exceed the daily recommended amount of 300mg.

Lipoproteins

Plasma carries fat and cholesterol around the body via the body's own transport system. Because these substances are not water-soluble, lipoproteins are their main carriers. Initially, after digestion and absorption, chylomicrons transport cholesterol, and upon leaving the liver, different lipoproteins continue distributing cholesterol to the cells of the entire body. These types of lipoproteins are determined by their density, and we refer to LDL as having low density and HDL as having high density. Too much LDL in the blood leads to deposits along the blood vessel walls, which in turn leads to arteriosclerosis (stiffening of arteries).

That's why LDL is described as the unwanted or 'bad' cholesterol, especially oxidised LDL which accelerates the formation of arteriosclerosis. You can prevent oxidation by eating fresh fruit and vegetables, which contain sufficient amounts of antioxidants.

While it is proven that an egg yolk contains 250mg of cholesterol, total cholesterol levels don't increase when consumed. The latest research shows that the substance lecithin contained in egg yolk is responsible for lowering blood cholesterol levels. For people who suffer from raised cholesterol levels, there is no issue with eating eggs. Diabetics, however, should not eat more than one chicken egg per day.

The HDL is considered the desirable or 'good' cholesterol, because it does not distribute cholesterol to other cells. Instead, HDL absorbs cholesterol and ensures its return to the liver.

Memory aid: Remember that the HDL value should be high, and the LDL value should be low. It is your goal to lower your LDL cholesterol levels and at the same time increase your HDL cholesterol levels. You can easily achieve this goal by applying the cholesterol elimination strategy. The reason this strategy should be your first choice is that most other lipid lowering treatments simultaneously decrease LDL as well as HDL values.

An Overview of Blood Lipid Values

Blood lipid values including total cholesterol, HDL, LDL, and triglycerides should be measured at least once a year. If these values are high, then it's important to carry out a control test after three months. Nowadays, tests can be carried out not only at GPs' surgeries but at many pharmacies too. Testing kits that allow you to measure cholesterol levels at home are also available from pharmacies.

The following values should be used as guidance:

Total cholesterol	< 200 mg/dl
LDL	< 160 mg/dl
HDL	at least 45 mg/dl
triglyceride	< 200 mg/dl

Strict guidelines concerning LDL and triglyceride values exist for diabetics and people suffering from high blood pressure because of the associated risk factors for cardio-vascular disease. We have only learnt recently, barely ten years ago, that elevated triglyceride values present a higher risk for cardiovascular disease. Today we know that we are dealing with another factor that, combined with high cholesterol levels, increases the risk of heart attacks. Being overweight and having diabetes are considered the main causes for elevated triglyceride blood levels.

Elevated Cholesterol Values

Several risk factors for cardio-vascular disease cannot be changed; these include hereditary predisposition and age. However, other factors can be influenced and include: smoking, high blood pressure, obesity, diabetes and high cholesterol values. Even slightly raised cholesterol values significantly increase the risk of suffering a heart attack. If cholesterol values rise above 300 mg/dl, this risk may triple.

This may sound alarming at first, but the good news is that we know that only ten percent of those adults have a total cholesterol level higher than 300 mg/dl. Although many pharmaceutical companies resist this message, we can be reassured that most people suffering from high cholesterol levels can be treated successfully by changing their eating habits and lifestyle.

In many cases, nutritionists agree that lipid-lowering drugs are unnecessary, and that without question the first approach for treatment should be a lipid-lowering diet. There are actually only very few patients with very high cholesterol levels who actually need lipid-lowering drugs. In any case, there are very few people who would not experience even a small change as a result of switching diets.

Remember that you need to have patience when waiting for the cholesterol-lowering effects of a change in diet. There is no quick-fix, and you need to wait at least eight to twelve weeks before you should recheck your blood values.

Dietary Change and Exercise

A healthy lifestyle and diet usually has a positive influence on blood lipid values, but unfortunately supermarkets harbour many dangers in the form of ready-made meals, alcohol and soft drinks. We know that each person uses up 1764lbs of food per year, and it seems obvious that in the light of this enormous amount, we should pay attention to the combination of foods we eat. The person suffering from high cholesterol levels needs to eat sufficient amounts of plant foods as opposed to animal-based foods, because of the obvious advantages of a cholesterol free diet.

Carbohydrates Influence Blood Lipid Values

Carbohydrates, especially sugar and high-sugar foods can raise triglyceride levels. This is also true for sugar substitutes like fructose. However, sweeteners are different and have no influence on either cholesterol or triglyceride levels as they don't belong to the group of carbohydrates. Foods that have a low glycaemic index either have no effect or can actually lower triglyceride levels.

Please, be aware of the concentration of sugar or fructose in drinks. You will take in a large amount of sugar very quickly if you drink a lot of fruit juice, nectar or lemonade. You need not worry if you drink mineral water to which you can add some lemon juice, or unsweetened tea with added artificial sweeteners to cover your daily recommended amount of 2 liters. Water-soluble fiber can also reduce cholesterol blood levels, especially plantago ovata seed husk; moreover, small amounts of fiber combine fats.

Research has shown that the glycaemic index (GI) can explain cardiovascular risks. The GI value shows how quickly carbohydrates can raise your blood sugar levels. With the exception of isolated fructose or fructose found in drinks, foods that indicate a low glycaemic index are a vital part of a healthy diet. Particularly recommended are, for example, whole wheat bread, oats, wheat bran, grain, legume, fresh vegetables, fruit (apart from those with high sugar content such as grapes or bananas), milk and milk-based products.

Proteins: Taking a Detour Effect

Proteins don't have an immediate effect on blood lipid values, but foods rich in protein often contain more fat. There are plenty of saturated fatty acids in animal foods such as meat and milk. If you have high cholesterol levels, you should try to replace animal proteins with plant proteins.

If you fancy Spaghetti Bolognese, you could join the many converts to spicy soya mince products, which are available from health food stores or organic food shops and are easy to use and perfect for beginners.

Why don't you try soya sausage or tofu instead of sausage or meat, and make a point of including soya products as well as soya drinks in your weekly food plan? This way you can lower your LDL cholesterol value significantly. In fact, studies have shown that soya can lower cholesterol levels by 10 percent, for example from 220 to 200 mg/dl. Bear in mind that this result was achieved without any other change in diet or taking any cholesterol reducers.

The Importance of Quantity and Quality

A large proportion of fat in our diets is derived from animal products and ready-made meals; the result is that our daily intake is made up of many saturated fatty acids and trans-fatty acids that have a negative influence on cholesterol-and triglyceride levels. However mono, as well as polyunsaturated fatty acids and phytosterols lower blood lipid values, while Omega-3 lowers triglyceride levels. The aim is to reduce the fat amount in total, but also to be mindful of the quality of the fat.

Saturated fatty acids: Palm kernel and coconut fat, butter, lard, fat meats, cold meat, cream.

Monounsaturated fatty acids: Olive oil, goose and duck lard, rapeseed oil, sesame seed oil.

Polyunsaturated fatty acids: safflower oil, flaxseed oil, rapeseed oil, nut oil, sunflower oil, low-fat margarine.

50 Ways to Lower Cholesterol Naturally

The following chapter contains 50 of the most important natural and side-effect free cholesterol reducing measures, which include food, dietary supplements and behavioural methods.

In most cases, a simple dietary change can reduce cholesterol values up to 300 mg/dL. Should blood lipid values rise above that, the usual medication dosage can often be reduced to a minimum if natural cholesterol reduction methods are used effectively.

Have a look at the following pages at the cholesterol reducing options that we suggest. Choose from fresh fruit and vegetables, fiber-rich grains and legumes. You will find high quality, plant-based proteins from low-fat milk products, fish, soya products and lean meats.

Throughout this chapter we have made an effort to provide practical tips as well as scrumptious recipes that you can use to help reduce your cholesterol levels, naturally.

When you prepare your meals, please make sure you use high-quality oils in small amounts, because ideally you should not exceed a total amount of 2-3oz of fat per day. Drink plenty of water and try to avoid sugary drinks.

Eventually your meals will become more and more healthy and cholesterol-friendly. After two to three months you can go to your doctor or pharmacy for a cholesterol check-up and notice the success of your new eating regime. It is actually possible to reduce cholesterol levels by 30-40 percent simply by changing your diet and including a targeted regime of cholesterol reduction.

Almonds

In the last few years the results of large-scale studies highlight the fact that injustice has been done to nuts, seeds and almonds by describing them as 'calorie bombs'. Some studies even show that almonds can make it easier to lose weight if consumed as part of a weight loss diet. The general rule 'one calorie equals one calorie' does not seem to apply here.

Almonds have few saturated fatty acids and plenty of mono-and polyunsaturated fatty acids, as well as fiber, Vitamin E and secondary plant products. One could describe almonds as a real cocktail of cholesterol fighters.

The composition is so unique that people suffering from high cholesterol levels and those at risk of heart attacks can eat them daily. It is not clear what specific ingredient it is in almonds, or which combination of ingredients is responsible for the LDL lowering effect. Yet we are sure that almonds reduce the risk of cardio-vascular problems significantly.

For the desired effect, about 1-1.5oz of almonds would be sufficient. Ideally, you want to eat nuts and almonds fresh, not roasted in oil, and they should be unsalted.

Spanish Spiced Whole Almonds

Serves 12

These kind of roasted almonds are really delicious and crispy along with offering a low cholesterol alternative for snacking. The spices along with brown sugar increase the astonishing taste of the almonds. This is an excellent snack food and if you have visitors this tasty snack food will fill the needs of absolutely everybody.

Ingredients:	Notes:	Measurements
Cumin	Ground	2 teaspoons
Paprika		1 teaspoon
Thyme leaves	Dried	1 teaspoon
Brown sugar	Light	1/4 cup
Kosher salt	-	1 teaspoon
Cayenne pepper	-	1/4 teaspoon
Water	-	1 tablespoon
Egg white, large	Large	1
Almonds	Whole and raw	2 cups

Directions:

1. Pre-heat the stove to 300°F

2. Cover a substantial rimmed cooking sheet using non-stick aerosol.

3. Stir cumin, paprika, thyme, brown sugar, salt and cayenne inside of a sizeable mixing bowl.

4. Stir egg whites along with the water inside of a low to medium dish until such time as they become frothy.

5. Incorporate almonds and blend in order to cover the almonds, strain via a strainer to remove excessive egg whites.

6. Blend the almonds into your dish filled with seasoning until eventually they are sufficiently covered.

7. Distribute equally onto the prepared cooking sheet.

8. Cook your almonds for 1.5 hrs. or more.

9. Stir every 30 minutes and cook them just till the almonds are generally free of moisture and golden brown. Cool completely and store in an air-tight container.

Antioxidants

Antioxidants (oxidation inhibitors) occur naturally in foods and prevent a reaction between delicate molecules and oxygen. Mostly they catch free radicals. We know that LDL cholesterol principally promotes the formation of arteriosclerosis. According to more recent scientific studies we know that oxidised LDL is particularly damaging.

Macrophages belong to the ingesting cells of the immune system and readily absorb oxidised LDL and keep it in storage. The high fat charge of macrophages results in the formation of foam cells that is believed to be the cause in the development of arteriosclerosis.

While lowering LDL cholesterol levels is vital, you should avoid LDL oxidation. You can avoid this by providing your body with effective antioxidant compounds. Vitamins E and C as well as secondary plant materials from groups such as carotenoids and flavonoids play an important role in this. It is also worth pointing out that trace elements such as zinc and selenium are effective in fighting oxidation of LDL cholesterol.

Eat a lot of fruit and vegetables in order to ensure your body is sufficiently provided with antioxidants. You can increase the bioavailability in your body by eating raw as well as cooked fruit and vegetables. You could also drink fresh juice, particularly tomato juice, if you are worried that your daily intake of oxidation inhibitors may not be sufficient.

You could also add naturally concentrated brewing yeast, sea buckthorn or rose hip concentrate. Try and eat five portions of fruit and vegetables per day. If you can manage to eat a colorful and varied mix you will provide your body with essential ingredients including antioxidants.

Good sources of antioxidants are, for example:

Vitamin E: Nuts/almonds, seeds, wheat germ oil, corn oil, sunflower oil, soybean oil, high-quality margarine.

Vitamin C: Oranges, lemons, grapefruit, clementines, currants, raspberries, sea buckthorn, kiwi, pepper, fennel, parsley, tomato.

Carotenoids: Tomato, pepper, broccoli, Brussels sprouts, kale, spinach, carrots, sweet corn, apricots, peaches, oranges.

Flavonoids: cherries, plums, red berries, apples, red cabbage, onions, radishes, radicchio, endive lettuce, aubergines.

The intake of a high dose of vitamin and mineral supplements may not be useful, and can be potentially damaging. A high intake of antioxidants may lead to a process that accelerates oxidation rather than achieving the opposite effect.

Apples

Good quality apples are widely available throughout the year and when bought fresh, lower blood lipids with no side-effects. This is mainly due to its high pectin content.

Many people are used to eating apples anyway because this handy snack also has a delicious taste. Some may find eating a large amount of apples daunting, and resort to apple pomace or concentrated pectin, which is available at health food stores or organic food shops. This way they don't miss out on the cholesterol-lowering effects.

It is even easier to use pectin preservative, but remember to check how much pectin is contained in the product you buy. If you want to lower your cholesterol levels by about 10 to 15 percent, you can achieve this by taking a daily amount of 0.01 to 0.02oz of pectin for three months. You will find that this is particularly effective in reducing the LDL value that is so damaging to your blood vessels, while the HDL value remains constant. By the way, quince has the highest pectin concentration of all foods. However, they should not be eaten raw, because they have a bitter taste and aren't easy to digest.

Hot Buttered Apples

Serves 2

This delicious and healthy recipe will get your family to eat their breakfast cereal! Add a small amount to any breakfast cereal for a fast and delicious treat!

Ingredients:	Notes:	Measurements
Red delicious, Golden Delicious or Granny Smith Apple	Large	1
Honey		1 ½ tablespoons
Butter		1 ½ teaspoons
Raisins		1 ½ teaspoons
Cinnamon	To taste	

Directions:

1. Remove the core from the apple

2. Slice the apple into thin slices

3. Combine the apple with honey, butter, and raisins into a small to medium sized microwavable bowl.

4. Apply cinnamon to taste

5. Cover the microwavable bowl with wax paper and cook on a high heat for approximately 90 seconds or till the apples are cooked yet firm.

Tips & Suggestions:

- For each apple used you can feed 2 people as a supplemental dish

- Experiment by adding to cereal, oatmeal, and granola or by itself.

Arginine

Amino acids are the smallest building blocks of proteins, and arginine is one of them. Different studies show that arginine has vital effects in the treatment of cardio-vascular diseases. This is because arginine cannot only maintain blood vessel elasticity, but also curbs the effect of platelet and white blood cell clumping, and thus prevents any blood congestion in the arteries.

The best food sources for arginine are nuts and almonds, sesame and wheat germ. You will also find respectable amounts in fish, meat, eggs and grain. The highly effective results that nuts and almonds show in lowering cholesterol are not just due to the high content in unsaturated fatty acids and Vitamin E, but also due to the arginine content that is responsible for this tasty cholesterol reducer.

In a widely acknowledged study, American scientists have shown that a daily intake of almonds can reduce cholesterol levels by about seven percent. Other studies show even better results when patients took pure arginine supplements; there was a decrease in cholesterol levels of up to ten percent. Fortunately, HDL-cholesterol serum levels are not influenced by arginine, but LDL levels are reduced, so that the HDL-LDL ratio is improved in favour of the good HDL value. For a sufficient supply you should have a daily intake of the arginine. Consult your doctor about the possibility of a supplement.

Handy Hint: Take a handful of almonds, walnuts, peanuts or hazelnuts and put them in your bag. Eat them when you feel like having snack. These can be very filling.

Artichokes

Traditionally, artichokes are starters because they facilitate diges-tion after a heavy main course. Nowadays we are much better informed about the positive properties of artichokes and we know that it contains a cocktail of substances that stimulate the gall bladder and the liver. Their effects on cholesterol levels are two-fold: the cynaroside agent inhibits an enzyme that is responsible for cholesterol production in the liver: effectively this means the body can only produce little amounts.

Secondly, the artichoke extract acts as a stimulant in the liver and gall bladder and leads to greater bile production that aids the digestion of fat in the gut. And last but not least, artichoke extract has antioxidant properties, which means we reduce the amount of oxidised LDL cholesterol.

According to the latest research, oxidised LDL cholesterol is a key factor in causing arteriosclerosis. Artichoke extract can contribute to the maintenance of normal cholesterol levels, and reduce the total as well as the LDL cholesterol values by about 20 percent.

Handy Hint: To achieve the desired cholesterol-lowering effect, we advise buying your artichoke extract from the pharmacy or health food store as with fresh ones will not have the same cholesterol-lowering outcome. Many people report that combining dietary fiber and artichoke, as well as artichoke concentrate and plantago ovata seed husk is sufficient in reducing cholesterol levels to normal.

Cheesy Baked Artichokes

Serves 4

This tasty dish is meant to be used as a healthy alternative to au gratin potatoes and is moist, cheesy and delicious and best'o!

Ingredients:	Notes:	Measurements
2 Packages of artichoke hearts	Frozen	18 ounces
Pecans	Ground	3 tablespoons

Parmesan Cheese	Grated	2 tablespoons
Dried Italian Seasoning	Crushed	1 teaspoon
Garlic Clove	Minced	1
Lemon Juice		1 tablespoon
Extra Virgin Olive Oil		1 teaspoon

Directions:

1. Pre-heat your cooker to 375°F

2. Cover the inside surface of a 9 inch glass pie pan with non-stick spray.

3. Put the frozen artichokes into a strainer

4. Rinse the artichokes with cool water to split up.

5. Strain water from the artichokes completely

6. Dry artichokes with a dry paper towel.

7. Pour into the already prepared pie pan. Sprinkle the tops of the artichokes with the lemon juice.

8. Combine the pecans, cheese, Italian seasoning, garlic, and oil in a small to medium sized bowl.

9. Distribute a combination consistently covering the top of the artichokes.

10. Cook for A quarter-hour, or simply up until the top is a light golden brown.

Beta-glucan

Beta-glucan is a natural food ingredient that belongs to the group of polysaccharides. There are larger amounts found in oats and oat products, for example, flakes, bread, crisp bread, mushroom and baking yeast. Mushrooms take on a special role, because they contain a highly-effective quality mix of different beta-glucan.

Recent research shows that beta-glucan is extremely suitable in preventing arteriosclerosis. Cholesterol levels are lowered and the LDL-HDL ratio is improved by the effect of beta-glucan on lowering the LDL value and improving the HDL value minimally.

The latest studies also point to the positive effect beta-glucan has on stimulating the immune system. If you want to be sure you get a sufficient amount of beta-glucan daily then use a brewing yeast product.

Blackberries

Blackberries belong to the rose family and grow along thorny tendrils. The leaves and blackberry fruits have been used ever since the days of Hippocrates for medicinal purposes. In comparison to other berries, the nutritious value of blackberries is its abundance in provitamin A and E. It delivers higher quantities of minerals including magnesium, calcium and iron than other fruit. Blackberries also contain potassium, vitamin C, copper and manganese, and they even have high fiber content.

The particular, their cholesterol reducing properties are related to their high content in flavonoids that have antioxidant effects. Flavonoids belong to the group of secondary plant materials that contain thousands of substances found in fruit, vegetables, legumes and grain. They are also known for their positive health effects, for example, on the regulation of blood sugars and cholesterol levels, as well as blood pressure.

Anthocyanins are plant pigments that are responsible for the purple color of blackberries. They strengthen the immune system and have anticarcinogenic properties. Blackberries also promote blood circulation, protect blood vessels and lower blood pressure.

Adding to this, one subgroup of flavonoids called polyphenols have special health benefits due to their component parts, ellagic acid and phenolic acids. The antioxidant effects are even 40 percent higher than that of an equivalent Vitamin E dosage. The blood velocity improves, while the LDL cholesterol value decreases and the HDL value increases.

Additional benefits: Flavonoids have anti-inflammatory effects and prevent tumours, venous diseases and haemorrhoids.

Recioie: Stewed Blackberries

Serves 4

This recipe tastes great when served on top of your favorite variety of low fat ice cream!

Ingredients:	Notes:	Measurements
Blackberries		4.5 cups
Water		½ cup
Salt	Pinch	
Sugar		½ cup

Directions:

1. Wash blackberries in cool water

2. Drain blackberries thoroughly

3. Place the blackberries to a medium sized pot

4. Insert the water and cover the pot with a tight fitting lid

5. Turn the heat to low and simmer the blackberries for approximately 15 minutes

6. Stir the berries every few minutes to prevent them from scorching.

7. Pour in the sugar and salt and stir together thoroughly

8. Heat blackberries over a low heat setting for an additional two to three minutes.

9. Take the pan off of the stove and allow it to sit and cool for about 10 minutes.

Tips & Suggestions

- You can either enjoy these warm or cool whichever you prefer.

- Try serving with cream for a delightful treat!

- If the blackberries that you are using are very ripe incorporate 1 tablespoon of lemon juice for flavor

Body weight

Towards the final chapter we present the most effective cholesterol lowering method: a few pounds less weight and daily exercise is highly effective in reducing your blood lipid levels. Each extra pound can bear heavily on your metabolism. Remember that weight loss reduction should be sustained and that crash diets and fasting can often lead to a so-called 'Yo-yo effect'. This is unsuitable for long-term and sustained weight loss; moreover, it is damaging to your heart, blood vessels and metabolism.

For people who are overweight, weight loss measures are one of the highest quality cholesterol reducing methods. Being overweight causes the development of metabolic disorders, arteriosclerosis, heart attacks and stroke. Usually losing about 5-10 percent of the base weight is sufficient to change the LDL and triglyceride values significantly. Nowadays, the Body-Mass-Index (BMI) is used to evaluate your body weight. There are a number of easy to use calculators online, which can aid you in calculating your BMI, or you can see your local GP who should also be able to assist you.

People who have a high body-mass-index should lose weight slowly and gradually. Nutrition experts recommend a weight loss target of one to two pounds per week. Crash diets that promise the loss of several pounds per week are not suitable for long-term weight loss. Don't be disheartened if your cholesterol levels rise during your diet program. In the long run cholesterol levels will lower to its original value and then be reduced even further.

Cholesterol levels will benefit from weight reduction, and all other health problems related to the metabolic syndrome (overweight, metabolic disturbances, high blood pressure and insulin resistance) will benefit from weight reduction as well. Insulin resistance will be reversed, blood pressure falls, and blood lipid levels improve.

Handy Hint: Predominantly choose low-fat protein suppliers: quark, 'Harzer' cheese, low-fat milk products, and fish and soy products. Carbohydrate supplies with a large component of dietary fiber fill you up for longer: whole wheat bread, legumes, cereals, fresh fruit and vegetables are good choices.

Use small amount of high-quality vegetable fats and avoid saturated fatty acids as much as possible. Remember to exercise, which will stimulate metabolism and more calories will be burnt.

Much loved habits are not broken easily. But step by step you can achieve your goal to consume cholesterol lowering items into your daily food plan, and to lose weight steadily over time.

Bread drink

For many hundreds of years, bread drink (Kwas) has been produced in Russia from rye, water and malt with about one percent of alcohol. Modern 'Kanne' bread drink is alcohol-free made from special whole grain sourdough bread and fresh spring water. You can get bread drink from health food stores, organic health food shops and large supermarkets.

What make this an excellent cholesterol reducing choice, are the probiotic lactic acid bacteria (Laktobacillus reuteri). They are responsible for the change in the gut flora, which causes the excretion of cholesterol contained in the bile. Bread drink provides one of the few opportunities for people suffering from milk protein allergy or lactose intolerance to get probiotics.

Handy Hint: Put 1/2 cup of bread drink and 1/2 cup of tomato juice in a large glass and add one teaspoon of oat bran as well as half a teaspoon of finely chopped pumpkin seeds. As garnish, use one stem of parsley and put it in the glass. Or you could use two to three cocktail tomatoes on a wooden skewer and place it on the edge of the glass.

Research has shown that there is a reduction of the total cholesterol level of up to 15 percent. To achieve this, you should drink a small glass of bread drink three times a day. It can be consumed on its own or mixed with mineral water. You can mix it with fruit or vegetable juice for quenching your thirst. You can also use bread drink to create creamy dips or quark, or to dilute in thick creamy soups.

Chicken eggs

Many people refuse to eat eggs for breakfast because they have a reputation of raising cholesterol levels. American scientists however have proven many years ago that this is complete fiction and that cholesterol levels remain constant even if you eat more than one egg per day. Many nutrition experts are of the opinion that eggs, milk and soy products belong to the most wholesome foods that are available to us. Contrary to popular belief chicken eggs don't present any risks to people with high cholesterol levels, instead they may have cholesterol lowering effects.

While one egg yolk provides a total daily amount of cholesterol, the body cannot absorb it all, because its absorption is hindered by lecithin also contained in the egg yolk. The arrangement of fatty acids in chicken eggs is similar to the of low-fat margarine. Don't hesitate to eat one egg every morning combined with fiber-rich whole wheat bread: it is a cholesterol-friendly breakfast that will fill you up for longer.

Handy Hint: You can now buy Omega-3 eggs or DHA eggs. Chicken receive a special seaweed supplement that leads to a change in the egg yolk's arrangement of fatty acids that effects a change in favour of Omega-3 fatty acid. According to the manufacturer, eating one of these eggs per day covers your daily recommended amount of this acid by about 40 percent.

Oatmeal Cottage Cheese Pancakes

Serves 1

If you are looking for a healthy treat that is almost too good to be true; you have got to try this recipe! These oatmeal cottage cheese pancakes are packed full of calcium, fibre and protein which make them not only delicious but nutritious as well!

Ingredients:	Notes:	Measurements
Oatmeal	Dry	1 Cup
Cottage Cheese		½ cup
Vanilla		1 teaspoon
Eggs	Whites Only	4

Directions:

1. Add all ingredients into the blender

2. Blend on low speed for approximately 30 seconds or until all ingredients are thoroughly blended

3. Add non-stick cooking spray to the inner surface of a large skillet.

4. Add batter to the pan until it forms a pancake that is approximately 3 inches in diameter

5. Flip once the top of the surface begins to bubble

6. Remove from pan once cooked throughout

7. Add your favorite toppings and enjoy!

Tips & Suggestions

- Eat them plain or with your favorite jam on top if you prefer!

- Add a small amount of orange or perhaps lemon zest before serving for a unique flavour experience!

Chrome

Chrome is a vital trace element that is firmly established in nutritional medicine. It influences the metabolism of carbohydrates, protein and lipids, but these mechanisms are not fully understood.

Nutrition scientists stipulate that the daily recommended amount should be between 30 to 100 µg per day. This is not what most of the population can achieve. To get a cholesterol lowering effect we need much larger amounts of chrome. This could then lower triglyceride and LDL-cholesterol levels in the blood, the HDL value would rise and the development of arteriosclerotic plaques be diminished.

You need at least 200 to 400 µg to achieve this. This can hardly be achieved with the help of food that only provides between 10 to 100 µg chrome per 1/4 pound, such as is the case with grain, legumes, nuts and meat. Nutritional supplements that you can get over the counter in any pharmacy can be of help.

Cinnamon

The polyphenol compound called MHCP is a secondary plant substance and the active ingredient responsible for the cholesterol lowering effect in this aromatic spice. Besides its pronounced effect on blood sugar levels, it has an excellent effect on blood lipid levels. One study examining its impact in Type 2 diabetics resulted in a decrease of cholesterol levels by about 12-26 percent after a month or so, the LDL value decreased by about 27 percent, and triglyceride levels decreased by up to 30 percent.

Please, make sure you get good quality cinnamon. When compared with cheap Cassia cinnamon, the Ceylon cinnamon shows fewer side-effects in terms of allergies and has fewer of the disputed ingredient coumarin. The more fine tasting Ceylon cinnamon does not overpower in taste even in large amounts, and is highly suitable for sweets and hearty meals. To ease consumption of the very valuable cinnamon spice, you might want to consider buying cinnamon capsules from the health food store or at the pharmacy.

Handy Hint: Half a teaspoon a day can achieve surprising results as far as cholesterol levels are concerned. Add plenty of cinnamon to muesli, yoghurt, quark and fruit salads. Even coffee and tea benefit in taste from a pinch of cinnamon. It does not have to be sweet all the time: many hearty Indian, Turkish and Greek dishes use cinnamon.

Baked Banana with Cinnamon & Honey

Serves 1

If you are looking for a delicious way to cut down on wasted bananas due to them becoming too ripe, this is an excellent delicious and nutritious recipe that will do just that!

Try adding this tasty treat to ice cream, cereal, oatmeal, porridge or even on its own you will love it!

Ingredients:	Notes:	Measurements
Banana	Ripe	1
Honey		2 teaspoons
Cinnamon	To taste	

Directions:

1. Turn on your oven and Pre-heat it oven to 390 F

2. Slice the banana up into small pieces or in half long ways

3. Place the cubed or sliced banana pieces onto a foil lined baking pan

4. Sprinkle cinnamon over the top to taste.

5. Pour the honey over the top of the banana evenly to coat

6. Bring the four corners of the foil inward and wrap together to trap steam inside.

7. Put into the oven for approximately 15 minutes or until the bananas are thoroughly heated.

Tips & Suggestions

- If you like your bananas a little firmer decrease your cooking time

- If you want the honey to caramelize then add a few minutes to the cooking time.

Co-enzyme Q10

The Co-enzyme Q10 has an important function in the maintenance of a healthy cardio-vascular system. The co-enzyme Q10 is also known as ubiquinone and is similar to different vitamins. Ubiquinone can be taken as part of your diet, and it is also provided by the human organism itself.

The most important function of the co-enzyme Q10 is the conversion of food energy into body energy. It also provides a protective shield against free radicals, and protects against LDL oxidation, as well as counteracting the effects of LDL-cholesterol deposits in the arteries.

Nutrition gives us 3-5 mg of co-enzyme Q10 every day. If you need a greater amount, or if you want to achieve a cholesterol lowering effect, you need to take ubiquinone food supplements with between 25 and 200 mg per day.

Handy Hint: The normal daily recommended amount of ubiquinone can be covered by eating meat, offal, fat-rich fish, nuts, legumes, sesame, sunflower seeds, vegetable oils, cabbage, onions, spinach, Brussels sprouts, potatoes and broccoli. For co-enzyme Q10 to work as a cholesterol reducer you require high dosages.

Dietary Fiber

For many centuries a large extent of our population adhered to a diet that was made up of fruit, vegetables, grain and legumes; however meat and sausages were only consumed from time to time. This is why there would have been an intake of up to 100 g of dietary fiber per day, without recognising its positive impact. Nowadays, food nutrition experts demand we should have at least 1/4 cup of dietary fiber per day, although many cannot achieve this.

Dietary fiber is an umbrella term that encapsulates plant products that cannot be used by the digestive system and are therefore passed through the body undigested. We differentiate between fiber types; insoluble fiber that does not dissolve in water, or soluble fiber which does dissolve in water. Insoluble fiber (also referred to as 'filling agents') binds with fluid and increase the volume in the intestine. The speed of the natural motion of the gut increases reducing the amount of time that chyme remains in the intestine. Water-soluble dietary fiber (also referred to as 'swelling agents') bind bile acids that largely consist of cholesterol as well as other metabolic materials which play a role in its excretion.

Pectin assumes a special status among dietary fiber. It is a natural component of cell walls and is used as a gelling agent when making jam. Different industries use pectin as a binding agent for gelling sugar, delicatessen sauces, mayonnaise, desserts, ice-cream, fruit mixes and sweets, for example fruit jelly.

Pectin is mostly gained from apple or orange peel or sugar beet pulp. It is certified E440 and has no upper quantity limit. A naturally high amount of pectin is found in quince, citrus fruits, apples, berries and carrots. A daily intake of only 6 to 10 g of pectin can have a cholesterol lowering effect.

The body needs cholesterol from the blood to produce new bile. Once cholesterol is absorbed from the blood, serum cholesterol and LDL levels fall. Water-soluble dietary fiber can reduce total cholesterol levels by about 10 to 15 percent, and the HDL component rises. Many studies confirm the cholesterol reduction effect of dietary fiber.

Exercise

LDL and total cholesterol levels can be reduced in part by many different cholesterol lowering methods. Important, however is the impact on HDL as well. In this case it is not about lowering the HDL level, but its increase. Most people's HDL levels are either borderline or too low. HDL may be described as a vessel cleaner; it keeps arteries free from calcifications and is even able to reduce existing arteriosclerosis.

By using different cholesterol lowering methods you can decease LDL and total cholesterol levels. If you want to effect a change in the LDL-HDL value ratio you should engage in sufficient exercise and endurance sports to raise the HDL cholesterol levels. Even if sports are not your favorite hobby you can easily think of a little exercise for the day.

Don't use the car for short routes (or long ones if you like), instead, take a walk or use your bike. Use the stairs instead of the lift. Get off the bus or the underground one or two stations in advance and go the rest of the way by foot. Park your car two blocks away from your flat and enjoy the rest of the evening by taking a short walk in the fresh air. This will benefit not only your cholesterol levels but also your body figure.

Handy Hint: Don't be misled by the term *endurance sports*. It merely means that you don't only need power but that you need to carry out your chosen type of sport over a longer period of time: you don't need to show high performance! Walking, hiking, cycling, swimming and rowing or canoeing are the types of sport that can be done by untrained people, they are fun and will be beneficial to your cholesterol levels. You should meet with like-minded people to feel motivated.

Flaxseed Oil

Virgin and cold-pressed flaxseed oil is a high-quality oil that has plenty of linoleic and linolenic acid. It is at the forefront of all plant-based oils. As such it is comparable with the classical supplier of Omega-3 fatty acids including salmon, herring and Mackerel.

Moreover, flaxseed oil is an anti-inflammatory, prevents thrombosis and has a positive effect on insulin levels. Unfortunately flaxseed oil is particularly susceptible to turning bitter, even after a few weeks when kept in ideal conditions.

Handy Hint: Never buy flaxseed oil in large quantities and always keep it in a dark and cool environment. It's best to keep it in a dark bottle or can. If you want to ensure that you consume it regularly, you could consider getting dietary supplements with flaxseed oil extracts. Specially treated oils are particularly tasty; its unique flavor, which is not to everybody's taste, is also slightly diminished.

Flaxseed oil is a perfect addition to the cholesterol-reducing-kitchen concept, which may include classical recipes for jacket potatoes with quark and flaxseed oil, or salad sauces for hearty dinner salads that could include lentils, beetroot, mushrooms,

green beans and strong lettuce like rocket, oak-leaf salad or dande-
lion.

Garlic

A diverse range of sulfur compounds in garlic makes it extremely
beneficial for the health of our blood vessels and metabolism.
These compounds belong to a group of so-called secondary plant
products. Garlic is very effective in lowering the total cholesterol
level and serum triglycerides. Moreover, it acts on widening blood
vessels and normalises our blood pressure.

Garlic can increase the HDL value, and reduce the LDL value as
well as inhibit cholesterol oxidation. If taken over long periods,
garlic can slightly reverse the formation of deposits (plaque) on the
inside of your arterial walls. This makes it a first class cholesterol
fighter. You have to be prepared to have at least 0.02 oz of garlic as
part of your daily diet, which is quite realistic, as garlic can be
eaten warm or cold. Only two cloves is a sufficient daily amount,
and you don't need to buy it ready-made.

Handy Hint: Combine a wholesome mix of important cholesterol
fighters including Vitamin E, sulfur compound and lecithin and
prepare a colorful vegetable stew, by frying tofu and garlic in a
little sunflower oil.

Research shows that a combination of garlic, Vitamin E and lecithin significantly lowers the LDL level. There is a synergistic
relationship between these substances. In other words, they com-
plement each other so that their combined impact is greater than
the sum of their individual parts.

Garlic Butter Rice

Serves 4

If you love using rice as a staple food and you also love garlic then this is the perfect side dish for you!

Ingredients:	Notes:	Measurements
Margarine or Butter	Use one or the other	1/3 cup
White or Jasmine Rice	Use one or the other	1/2 cup
Chicken Bouillon Cubes	To taste	1-2
Water or Chicken Broth	Use one or the other	1 ½ cups
Minced garlic	To taste	2-3 tablespoons

Directions:

1. Add the margarine or butter that you will be using into a large skillet

2. Turn on the burner to a medium heat setting

3. Allow the butter to cook until thoroughly melted

4. Pour the rice into the hot skillet with the butter

5. Stir the rice and butter together until the rice is evenly coated with butter or margarine

6. Add the bouillon cubes to the mixture and stir until they are dissolved

7. Turn down the heat to a low setting and allow the rice to cook for about 2-3 minutes

8. Add the water and stir

9. Cover with a tight fitting lid

10. Reduce the heat to the lowest heat setting

11. Allow all ingredients to simmer until it the mixture comes to a low boil this typically takes about 10 minutes

12. Remove the lid and add the minced garlic stirring until thoroughly blended

13. Replace the lid and cook for an additional five minutes or until the rice is the desired tenderness

Tips & Suggestions

- Feel free to play with the amount of water and garlic in the recipe depending on the moisture level and flavour that you prefer.

- Decrease the cooking time on the garlic in order to preserve the health benefits of the garlic.

- Serve plain, as a side dish or with eggs or try adding to any of your favorite rice dishes!

- If you are on a sodium controlled diet you can eliminate the chicken bouillon from the recipe and use water in place of chicken broth.

Glycine

Glycine is a building block for protein that, among many other benefits, also has a cholesterol reduction effect. The manufacture of bile acids is one of the most important ways in which cholesterol is excreted. As a conjugate of glycine or taurine it is excreted into the small intestine via the gall bladder, where they play a role in reabsorption of fats and fat-soluble vitamins.

About 0.05 oz of cholesterol is converted into bile acid in the liver every day, which is necessary for the absorption of fat into the small intestine. A large part of this bile acid will be reabsorbed in the gut and passed back to the liver. There is no excretion of bile acid. This is very important for a healthy person, because this reabsorption of bile acid into the liver is to ensure that cholesterol production in the body stays within normal limits.

The amino acid glycine is absolutely vital for this process. When cholesterol levels get too high, glycine can stimulate the body's own regulating mechanism. Glycine converts cholesterol into bile acid that is being excreted via the gut. If we have less bile acid being transported from the gut back to the liver, cholesterol production is then stimulated in the liver by the body itself. Because cholesterol is being utilised more as a source material, blood cholesterol levels decrease.

Powder or capsule supplements are available over the counter at the pharmacy. By the way, don't be surprised if you find glycine as an additive on the list of food ingredients. It has been certified as a flavour enhancer without any maximum quantity restrictions.

Guar

Guarseed flour is made from the Indian cluster bean. This legume has been firmly established in traditional medicine for decades, but has also been mentioned in scientific terms with respect to its treatment of raised blood lipid levels. The ground bean, for example, is used to treat diabetics and people suffering from weight problems.

The main component of the guar seed is water-soluble dietary fiber that successfully interferes in the bile acids' circulation in order to lower cholesterol levels. Guarseed flour is now available in organic food shops and health food stores. Guar is certified to be used as thickening-and gelling agents (referred to as E412), among others, in desserts, ice-creams, jams, soups and sauces.

Guar therapy however is started with a low dose, which you can increase over time. This helps to ease the load on the digestive tract. Guar requires a large amount of water to swell up; therefore, you should take it with lots of water.

Gugulipid

Gugulipid is found in the resin of a myrrh tree. For many centuries it has been part of ayurvedic medicine. Gugulipid lowers the vessel damaging LDL cholesterol and increases the good HDL cholesterol. The liver gets stimulated to produce bile acid and it promotes fibrinolysis of the blood (prevention of blood clumping, dissolving of blood clots).

We don't know very much about the side-effects of any long-term intake or overdose. Please consult your doctor about taking the appropriate product.

Kefir

Kefir originally comes from the Caucasus. Some people are known to drink Kefir because they want to maintain good health and live to old age.

Manufactured Kefir is generally offered in supermarkets in a mild form. The milk is treated with the same mix of different bacteria and yeast so that kefir always tastes the same. The complex effect of the natural kefir fungus cannot always be copied.

Kefir is incredibly healthy and has a cholesterol lowering effect. This is due to its high content in lactic acid bacteria and yeast that have probiotic effects. The cholesterol lowering effect is achieved by drinking half a liter of kefir daily. It also strengthens your immune system and protects against allergies and other sensitivities.

In the supermarkets, kefir is offered according to different levels of fat content. You should choose the low-fat version to avoid consuming too many calories. The cholesterol reducing effect sets in when you drink two glasses of kefir per day. Try and use fresh kefir and don't keep it for too long in the fridge. This way you can really reap the most benefit.

Handy Hint: If you drink kefir daily, consider buying your own kefir fungus. You will save on all the cost and packaging, and home-made kefir really is very aromatic in taste and quenches your thirst. Above all it is a great cholesterol fighter that exceeds the effects of a manufactured kefir drink. You can order kefir fungus over the Internet, and usually it comes with instructions.

L-carnitine

The need for the substance L-carnitine is partially covered by the body's own functions, but also by the consumption of meat and meat products. Lamb contains particularly high levels of carnitine. L-carnitine is responsible for the combustion of fatty acids in the energy cells called mitochondria. It may be necessary to take L-carnitine as a supplement, as in the case of a vegetarian diet, for example, or when on a low-fat diet where less meat and meat products are consumed.

L-carnitine lowers total cholesterol as well as the LDL levels while at the same time raising the HDL level. L-carnitine shows benefits in people with heart disease, cardiac arrhythmias or general heart weakness, and it influences the provision of an optimum amount of energy to heart muscle cells. In some countries it is used effectively as cardiac therapy. L-carnitine also shows benefits in sports professionals. In the U.S. it is used to prevent and treat cardio-vascular disease.

Lecithin

The name lecithin is derived from old Greek language egg yolk. Lecithin (phospholipids, lipamin) is a component of the cell membranes of animal and plant cell wall. The vital lipamin is generated by the body or via synthetic food processes. Lecithin acts as a solubiliser of food fats and cholesterol and is responsible for getting rid of the excess LDL cholesterol in the blood. It prevents arteriosclerosis, one of the most important risk factors for heart attacks. Lecithin's effect is equivalent to that of other pharmaceutical lipid lowering agents.

Many pharmaceutical companies and chemical groups don't want to hear this, but lecithin's effect is mentioned in numerous scientific studies. They show that lecithin has a special lowering effect on the LDL component by up to 30 percent, which is the part that is so damaging to the blood vessels, doing so without decreasing the HDL value at the same time.

Handy Hint: For the preparation of scrambled and fried egg you should cover your frying pan with little oil to avoid the additional calorie intake. Boiled or poached eggs are easily served without adding any calories.

If you want to take lecithin, you don't need to resort to lecithin-rich products from your pharmacy or health food store. Just one egg for breakfast will be sufficient to lower your cholesterol levels effectively. While the egg yolk contains up to 300 mg of cholesterol (depending on egg size), thanks to lecithin the total cholesterol amount will not be absorbed.

In addition, you should eat lecithin-rich soy and lupine products weekly. The beneficial effects of lupine are: it protects liver cells, supports the immune system, and protects the function of the brain. Lupine is effective if you suffer from low concentration, and studies have even shown its use for dementia and Alzheimer.

Macadamia Nuts

The Macadamia nut is described as the queen of all nuts and is a particularly tasty cholesterol reducer. This may be to do with the 70 percent fat content, which makes it the nut with the highest fat content.

However, the actual proportion of unsaturated fatty acids is about 80 percent, and the less desirable saturated fatty acids only make up 15 percent.

This favourable composition of fats is what makes the Macadamia nut have such a positive effect on cholesterol levels, on LDL cholesterol levels and on coronary heart disease. There are numerous studies testing nuts with at least 20 percent energy delivery that support these cholesterol lowering effects.

Macadamia nuts that are soft and palatable are rarely available to buy in the shell because they generally have very tough shells that cannot be easily opened with a common nut cracker.

Macadamia Nut Hummus

Makes 2.5 cups

This sweet and spicy Hawaiian themed humus is a great healthy snack that is excellent used as a dip or served as a spread on your favorite bread or bagel!

Ingredients:	Notes:	Measurements
Macadamia Nuts	Roasted	½ cup
Garbanzo beans	Drained	2 cups
Olive Oil		2 tablespoons
Lemon juice		1 tablespoon
Water		3 tablespoons
Garlic	Minced	1 teaspoon
Basil leaves	Medium Size	10

Directions:

1. Add each ingredient into a blender or food processor

2. Blend until smooth and thoroughly mixed

3. Remove from blender or food processor

4. Place into serving dish

Mackerel

Measuring between 30 and 50cm, this shoaling fish is predominantly found in the coastal waters of North America and Europe. Compared to salmon, it is considered one of the cheaper cholesterol fighters. Triglyceride total cholesterol and LDL levels are reduced because of the high Omega-3 fatty acid content in mackerel, herring and the like, and the good HDL cholesterol levels increase. The amount of Omega-3 fatty acid found in fish is dependent on the catchment area and the type of food that is given to the animals. That's why you find different figures being quoted on different fatty acid value tables.

However, mackerel, herring, tuna, sardines and salmon are the fish types that are on top of these value tables: they show values of over 1.5 g Omega-3 fatty acids per 100g. Lean sea fish contains only about 0.3 g.

Fish can of course provide a healthy main course, when fried, steamed or baked. Fifty to 100g of fish per day is sufficient to achieve the cholesterol lowering effect.

The following can be used instead of cold meats and cheese for a hearty evening meal: Peppered mackerel, sardines, herring fillets, Bismarck Herring, rollmops and herring in jelly or tomato sauce. You can create a complete cholesterol-friendly meal by adding strips of smoked or stained graved salmon, or drained canned tuna to soups or make a colorful salad dish. In the former East Germany there was a triglyceride lowering mackerel diet. The positive impact of regular consumption of mackerel exceeds that of too many drugs that currently exist to treat high triglyceride values.

Mono-Unsaturated Fatty Acids

Almost all fats belong to the group of triglycerides, which are three fatty acids combined with glycerine. While fat is always high in calories, they don't all have the same mechanism. Some act as cholesterol fighters, while some actually raise cholesterol levels. Mono-unsaturated fatty acids belong to the group of cholesterol fighters and that's why you need not worry about the amount of fat content, but more so about the quality of the lard.

Ideally, you want to use foods that are barely saturated, and contain many mono and polyunsaturated fats in order to achieve a cholesterol lowering effect. Oleic acid belongs to the mono-unsaturated fatty acids and is predominantly found in rapeseed, sunflower, hazelnut and sesame oils.

You can potentially lower your cholesterol levels by up to 15 percent if you can replace the saturated fatty acids in your diet with mono-unsaturated fats. Mono-unsaturated fatty acids are less susceptible to oxidising than poly-unsaturated fatty acids. The latter would require plenty of healthy Vitamin E to protect it from oxidisation. The much hailed positive effect of the Mediterranean diet described in many studies is often related to the use of favourable oils and sea fish. In Southern cuisine we find less of the fatty meats with the unfavourable fat profiles than in our own.

Muesli

Muesli is a mix of different cholesterol fighters and provides for an ideal breakfast or snack for people who need to decrease their cholesterol levels or who need to prevent problems with their fat metabolism. Not all mueslis can lower cholesterol to the same degree: please, check the label for the amount of sugar and the sometimes small amounts of fiber. Breakfast cereals, mostly those classed for children's breakfast have little to do with muesli and should be classed as 'sweets'.

Handy Hint: Oats are perfect ingredients for the anti-cholesterol-muesli, as well as oat bran, flax seed, dried apricots and cranberries, walnuts, sesame seed, sunflower seeds, almonds, pistachios and cinnamon. You get the most from muesli when grating an apple (with the apple peel), and a little freshly pressed orange juice and low-fat kefir.

There are some health food shops where you can have your muesli mixed. But we recommend you buy small amounts often, as keeping large amounts of muesli in storage is not worth it. Nuts, seeds and kernels could be damaged. Mix in fresh fruit with your muesli, especially the pectin-rich apple. Especially effective are the fiber-rich redcurrant berries or other berries as they contain antioxidants that are important micronutrients. Enjoy your muesli with a soya drink, low-fat milk or probiotic milk product. If consumed regularly, you can reduce your cholesterol levels by up to 15 percent.

Bircher Muesli

Serves 1

The Bircher Muesli was first created in the early 1900's as a nutritious dietary supplement that was high in fibre rich fruits and vegetables and was used as nutritional therapy to treat a variety of conditions! This mixture is both tasty and healthy while also providing you with a variety of vitamins and fibre for digestive health!

Ingredients:	Notes:	Measurements
Rolled Oats	Soaked in 2-3 tablespoons	1 tablespoon
Lemon juice		1 tablespoon
Cream		1 tablespoon
Large Apple	Grated	1
Ground hazelnuts or almonds	One or the other (optional)	1 tablespoon

Directions:

1. Place 2-3 tablespoons of water into a medium sized mixing bowl

2. Place rolled outs into the water and allow the oats to soak until softened

3. Add all of the other ingredients one by one into the bowl

4. Stir all ingredients until thoroughly combined

5. Enjoy alone or with low fat milk

Niacin

Niacin is a Vitamin B complex, previously described as Vitamin B3. It is an umbrella term for vitamers (chemically similar compounds) nicotinamide and nicotinic acid that can be transformed into one another within the organism. Niacin can be found in all living cells and is stored in the liver. The B-vitamin is an important building block for different co-enzymes and has a central function in the metabolism of fats, proteins and carbohydrates. Compared to other B-vitamins, nicotinic acid is less sensitive to heat, light and oxygen, so that any loss that occurs in its preparation is less than ten percent. Natural suppliers of niacin are poultry, wild game, fish, mushrooms, low-fat milk products and eggs, offal, whole wheat products, vegetables, fruit and nuts. Niacin from animal sources is basically utilised more efficiently.

A sufficient amount of niacin is also found in brewing yeast. The recommended niacin intake is dependent on age, weight and sex and varies between 13 and up to 17 g per day. This can usually be covered by a varied diet.

Its therapeutic dose of between 500 up to 1000mg can only be covered by dietary supplements. If you want to achieve a cholesterol lowering effect, you need to take large amounts of niacin per day. A significant reduction of the LDL cholesterol and triglyceride levels, as well as a significant HDL increase can only be achieved with a dosage of between 5000-1000 mg of niacin per day.

Oats

Oats have an unusual nutrient profile and a special status among other types of grain. Unfortunately it has become slightly out of fashion and is generally consumed as oat flakes. The oat grain has a high vegetable fat content and exceeds that of other grains by an average of seven to eight percent.

Its composition is particularly advantageous for high cholesterol levels: it contains 40 percent of linoleic acid, and 35 percent of oleic acid. Both fatty acids have preventative effects on the cardio-vascular system: if consumed regularly, they significantly lower LDL blood cholesterol levels and blood pressure. You can cover your daily recommended amount of linoleic acid and oleic acid with the help of the unsaturated fatty acids of the oat grain.

The oat's high fiber content gives you a feeling of being full for longer, and in addition, cholesterol content is reduced because of a slowing rate of absorption from the intestines; and bile production is also stimulated.

It really makes sense to eat oats in different varieties every day, and enjoy eating it, for example, as bread, roll or crisp bread. Oat seeds and oat flakes are very filling and they are great cholesterol reducers in cereals and fruit salads. When baking, you can replace up to 25 percent of wheat flour with fine oats, without having to change the recipe or baking time.

Golden Oats

Serves 2

This tasty dish can be used as a side dish or alone as a breakfast dish; and you can rest assured that it is as healthy as it is tasty with the reduced sodium and reduced calorie recipe.

You can also mix the dry ingredients ahead of time to take along with you when you need a quick and healthy meal on the go!

Ingredients:	Notes:	Measurements
Rolled whole oats	Uncooked	1 ½ cups
Egg	Beaten	1
Margarine or Butter	Use one or the other	1 ½ tablespoons
Water		¾ cup

Directions:

1. Add the margarine or butter to a medium sized sauce pan.

2. Heat margarine or butter over a medium-low heat until thoroughly melted.

3. Crack the egg into a small mixing bowl

4. Add the oats into the same small mixing bowl with the egg.

5. Mix the egg and oats together until the oats and egg are thoroughly combined

6. Pour the egg and oats mixtures into the heated skillet

7. Allow the oats to cook for about five minutes stirring consistently so that the oats are evenly browned

8. Make sure that the oats are dry to the touch and thoroughly separated

9. Add water and stir

10. Cover and allow the mixture to sit for about five minutes

Tips & Suggestions

- If you like you can store individual servings in sandwich baggies until ready to use.

Olive Oil

Cold-pressed olive oil of the highest quality contains even more oleic acid than rapeseed oil and therefore, is an effective LDL cholesterol lowering food. But we need to remember that the type of olive oil sold in supermarkets is often very different from that used in scientific studies, which are largely responsible for its positive image.

In many cases when cheap olive oil becomes available, it is not carefully cold-pressed, and instead, simply treated with water vapor. At professional tastings they are sometimes described as 'rancid' or 'moldy'. These oils are often wrongly labeled 'virgin' or 'extra virgin'. Its distinctive taste leads to a very limited use, and basically, it is only really suitable for Mediterranean cold dishes.

Unfortunately olive oil has been misunderstood as far as its cholesterol-lowering properties in large quantities are concerned. One of the key factors in fighting high blood lipid values is weight reduction. If you want to lower you LDL by means of a modified diet, you should use 2-3 tablespoons of oil per day, for overweight people we recommend only 1-2 tablespoons of oil.

Omega-3 Fatty Acids

In the middle of the last century scientists established that Eskimos rarely suffer from cardio-vascular diseases. Even then we presumed that this is due to the Eskimos' diet that is rich in fish. Today we know that fish fat has a high share of Omega-3 fatty acids, which belongs to the group of poly-unsaturated fatty acids.

They are absolutely essential and have to be consumed because our bodies don't produce these fatty acids. Eicosapentaenoic acid (EPA) and docosahexaenoic acid (DHA), as well as linolenic acid from vegetable oils belong to the cholesterol friendly fatty acids.

As far as Omega-3 fatty acids are concerned, many think of fish and seafood. Plant-derived alpha-linolenic acid also belongs to the group of Omega-3 fatty acids. Linolenic acid contains the highest proportion with about 50 percent of this fatty acid, but walnut, rapeseed and soya oil are equally valuable sources.

After you have consumed Omega-3 fatty acids, triglyceride levels initially fall by about 20-25 percent on average. But afterwards the whole lipid profile improves, LDL levels decrease and HDL levels increase. Total cholesterol levels decrease by about 10 percent. Few drugs are available to influence triglyceride levels, and that's why it is all the more important to reduce its risk in natural ways.

Oranges

The orange is known to be a healthy fruit: most people will think of Vitamin C and its antioxidant properties as useful in staving off winter colds. It also contains plenty of the water-soluble fiber pectin, which binds with cholesterol in the gut (deposited there with the help of bile acid) in order to be excreted. This form of cholesterol can no longer be reabsorbed in the body and is no longer available to the liver. As a result, cholesterol from the blood is utilised in order to produce new bile acid in the liver. For that to happen, LDL receptors are activated in the liver. Pectin is particularly responsible for lowering LDL that can do serious harm to blood vessels, instead of lowering the HDL.

Equally, all other citrus fruits contain a large amount of pectin. Therefore, they should form part of your regular diet. But unfortunately orange or grapefruit juice does not have the same advantage because the fiber-rich pulp often never, or only in small amounts ends up in the juice.

If you want to lower your LDL levels you need to consume two oranges per day or the equivalent amount of citrus fruits, for example clementines or grapefruit. However, you can also get pectin-based cholesterol-lowering food supplements.

Orangeade

Makes 1 gallon

This marvellous orangeade is a delicious drink that is super healthy and just as quick and easy to prepare! If you are searching for a healthy and thirst quenching summer alternative to lemonade then you just have to try orangeade!

Ingredients:	Notes:	Measurements
Oranges		5
Limes		3-4
Lemons		5
Water		3.5 liters
Sugar	Granulated	1 ¾ - 2 cups

Directions:

1. Cut oranges, lemons and limes into thin slices

2. Place the cut slices of fruit into a 1 gallon pitcher

3. Pour the sugar into the pitcher and allow it to sit for approximately 15 -30 minutes

4. Squeeze the juice from the fruit into the pitcher once the allotted time as passed

5. Rinse the squeezed slices of fruit with water to allow sugar to drain into the pitcher

6. Add water to the fruit juice and sugar mixture in the pitcher

7. Serve over ice

8. Garnish with citrus rinds if you prefer

Tips & Suggestions:

- You can add your favorite ingredients into the recipe as you wish. Some suggestions that are a tasty alternative are fresh fruit pieces, cinnamon.

Peanuts

Existing studies show that if we eat peanuts daily the risk of cardio-vascular illness, as well as total cholesterol levels and its LDL component are reduced. To date, it is not clear which specific ingredient is responsible for this cholesterol reducing effect. But scientists believe that the positive effect on the heart and blood vessels is probably due to the peanuts' high content in unsaturated fatty acid, as well as its low content in saturated fatty acid.

Daily consumption of peanuts lowers LDL values significantly, but also reduces triglycerides. Studies also show that daily consumption of peanuts raise HDL levels.

Interestingly, one particular study shows that people who consume nuts and oil crops regularly are general slimmer than those who try and avoid them, for example because of their high calorie content.

Thai Chicken Salad with Peanuts and Lime

Serves 4

This delicious chicken salad is the perfect addition to any summer cookout or picnic with its crunchy peanuts, zesty lime juice and flavourful seasonings this is not your ordinary chicken salad!

Ingredients:	Notes:	Measurements
Boneless skinless Chicken breasts	Cooked	2
Romaine lettuce	Chopped	4 cups
Cucumber	Diced	1 cup
Tomato	Diced	1 cup
Scallion	Chopped	½ cup
Chicken broth		1 cup
Peanut Butter	Creamy	2 tablespoons
Soy sauce		1 tablespoons
Sesame oil		2 teaspoons
Lime juice		2 tablespoons
Peanuts	Roasted	¼ cup

Directions:

Salad:

1. Place chopped romaine lettuce into a large mixing bowl

2. Sprinkle chopped chicken breasts evenly throughout the salad

3. Place the scallions, tomatoes and cucumbers which you have diced evenly into the salad as well

Dressing:

1. Add chicken broth, soy sauce, lime juice, peanut butter and sesame oil in a medium sized mixing bowl

2. Use a whisk to thoroughly combine all of the ingredients together

3. Pour the mixture over the top of the chopped romaine lettuce

4. Sprinkle peanuts over the top of the finished salad

Phytosterol

Phytosterol only appears in plant-derived foods and is quite similar in structure and function to that of cholesterol that is derived from animal products. Their structural similarity makes it possible for the body to prefer the plant substances to that of cholesterol. This means that cholesterol is excreted, the cholesterol cycle is interrupted, total cholesterol values are reduced by 10-15 percent, and the LDL value are reduced by about 5 percent. You need to consume about 0.05 to 0.11oz of phytosterol in order to achieve this result. Any dosage below 1 g rarely achieves any results. However, if more than 0.11oz is consumed, the cholesterol will not be reduced any further. If you were to overdose on phytosterol there would not be any health damage. In reality, we generally consume minute amounts of plant sterols: too little to influence cholesterol levels.

It is hardly possible to influence cholesterol levels by increasing the amount of phytosterol in our diet. In the table below you get an overview of the phytosterol content in foods.

Phytosterol food content

Food	Phytosterol content
Seeds and nuts	22–714 mg/100 g
Grain	1–200 mg/100 g
Vegetables	1–100 mg/100 g
Fruit	2–30 mg/100 g

Supplements or foods that are supplemented with phytosterol are more useful. Nowadays you can find low/half-fat margarines by different manufacturers, as well as dietary supplements, "Centrum Kardio", milk and special milk drinks, as well as yoghurt products that contain plant sterols that have therapeutic effects. Read the labels if you use different products. More often you will get the recommended daily amount of phytosterol in one yoghurt drink.

You will recognise cholesterol fighting products by searching for the reference "plant sterols/plant stanols additive" that should be found next to the product's name. The actual amount of phytosterols should be marked in the list of ingredients.

Pistachio

In a botanical sense, pistachios are not classified as nuts. However, they are commonly classified as nuts because they frequently have a very similar use and composition when compared with the 'classical nut'. Pistachios are rich in unsaturated fatty acids, and several studies have proven that a daily portion of pistachios can reduce total cholesterol levels. Pistachios have a higher proportion of antioxidants than almonds or nuts. Equally they have relatively high fiber content.

Plant fibers can reduce cholesterol levels effectively, especially its LDL component. In addition, pistachios have a high amount of phytosterols that are able to lower cholesterol absorption from our food intake: only 1/4 cup of pistachios daily, about a handful – are sufficient. At first you should weigh them properly rather than taking a rule of thumb measure. This is because while they are a great cholesterol fighter, you should also be aware that they are packed full of energy.

Fruit and Pistachio Salad

Serves 2

This wonderful, colorful and delicious fruit salad is a tasty treat by itself as a side dish or as the perfect addition to any summer barbeque or picnic!

Ingredients:	Notes:	Measurements
Pear	Red/Large	1
Honeydew melon		5 ¼ Ounces
Banana	Small	1
Passion Fruit	Pulp removed	2
Pistachios	Unsalted	10

Directions:

1. Cut the pear into small sized slices

2. Peel the honeydew melon and remove all seeds

3. Chop honeydew melon into bite sized pieces

4. Remove peel from banana and chop into bite sized pieces

5. Remove the pulp from the 2 passion fruits and cut the pulp of the fruit into small pieces

6. Stir all ingredients together in large mixing bowl until thoroughly blended

7. Top with pistachios just before serving

Poly-unsaturated fatty acids

Poly-unsaturated fatty acids are vital in the diet because they cannot be manufactured in the body and instead rely on a daily supply. Important representatives of this fatty acid are linoleic and linolenic acid. The double bonds of the poly-unsaturated fatty acids are very sensitive to chemical reactions with oxygen (oxidation).

Fortunately many healthy seeds and nuts contain oil that is rich in Vitamin E, which protects against oxidation. Fats with high poly-unsaturated fatty acid content are sensitive to heat and are therefore unsuitable for frying and deep-frying. Alternatives should be used as listed in the table below.

Alternatives to bad fats

Not suitable as cholesterol killer	Better choice
Salad oil	
Palm kernel oil	Flaxseed oil, Nut oil, safflower oil, Rapeseed oil, sunflower oil, seed oil, olive oil (all cold-pressed)
For frying:	
Coconut fat, Butter lard, pork lard	Refined rapeseed oil, refined sunflower oil
Bread spread	
Butter	Low-fat margarine

Butter and margarine are principally not useful for frying, please, always use vegetable oil.

Probiotics

Probiotics are generally understood to be specific microorganisms, often lactobacilli or bifidobacteria which have a particular health benefit in the gut flora. Probiotic foods like kefir or bread drink are able to act as cholesterol reducers.

Scientists have observed that lactic acid bacteria lower the cholesterol content in the respective food medium. That's why it was assumed that bacteria could be used to reduce serum cholesterol levels. This may be achieved on two levels: on one level lactic acid bacteria can bind and decompose cholesterol so that less of it can be absorbed from the intestine into the blood; on the other, probiotics are responsible for an increased excretion of bile acid. The production of new bile acid requires cholesterol from the blood which has a cholesterol-lowering effect.

Research results vary: while some describe moderate reductions in cholesterol values, others show good results. Other studies also point out the preventative benefits of probiotics. The cholesterol-lowering effect of lactic acid bacteria appear to strongly depend on its original source, the consumed amount and the cholesterol values of the participants.

Handy Hint: The number of living microorganisms that reach the gut undamaged is of utmost importance to achieve the desired effect. Probiotics, therefore, should be consumed as freshly as possible as the amount of effective germs is diminished the closer you get to the sell-by date. Probiotics should be consumed daily if you want to achieve a cholesterol lowering effect.

You need to ensure a constant supply of lactobacilli or bifidobacteria to the gut because they cannot reside there for long, and the germs are soon pushed out by other bacteria in the gut. Probiotic foods are particularly recommended after a treatment of antiobiotics that tend to destroy pathogens as well as bacteria in the gut. This way you quickly re-build a healthy gut flora.

Psyllium

Plantago ovata is part of the plantain populations and grows in India and Pakistan. Its seeds are generally referred to as psyllium.

Psyllium contains over 70 percent of water-soluble dietary fibers and is therefore the richest of all natural sources of this substance. It can lower cholesterol levels by 15 percent without showing any damaging side-effects. There are equivalent psyllium preparations available in pharmacies.

To achieve a cholesterol lowering effect, you should drink one glass of water or juice daily and mix it with one to two teaspoons of psyllium, either just before or with your meal. You can also simply sprinkle it on your muesli or yoghurt, as you would do with flax-seed. But don't forget that swelling agents like psyllium require plenty of fluids to achieve the desired effect. You should drink two to three liters daily.

Pumpkin Seed Oil

Pumpkin seed oil is tasty and healthy. The yellow-green seeds of the pumpkins that are harvested in autumn are the basis for this distinguished specialty. It originally comes from Austria, from a place called Steiermark. It takes about 5.5-6.5 pounds of pumpkin to gain 1 liter of Pumpkin seed oil. The seeds are ground, carefully roasted and pressed.

It has a wonderful nutty aromatic taste, and as part of this range of cholesterol fighters, it provides for a high share in phytosterols. The University of Graz has recently emphasised the potential use of pumpkin seed oil for antioxidant treatment. Similar to other oils, pumpkin seed oil should be kept at cool temperatures and in the dark, and used up within 6 months.

Pumpkin seed oil with the label 'g.g.A.' is protected by law and is guaranteed to come from Steiermark, Austrian.

Handy Hint: Pumpkin seeds and their oils contain all the properties of cholesterol fighters already mentioned. The culinary use of pumpkin seeds varies: finely chopped you could eat them raw and add them to salads, compote and cereals. Equally, you could add them to sweet dishes, cake or biscuits, which gives you a tasty alternative to nuts and almonds.

Rapeseed Oil

Rapeseed oil is one of the most important cholesterol lowering foods that you could possibly use in your kitchen. It is rich in unsaturated fatty acids and is perfectly balanced between mono- and polyunsaturated fatty acids. In fact, 90 percent of rapeseed oil consists of unsaturated fatty acids, which is the highest proportion out of all cooking oils. Noticeable is its high oleic acid content, which is one of the simple mono-unsaturated fatty acids. Oleic acid can reduce LDL cholesterol levels without simultaneously lowering HDL cholesterol. Linoleic acid and Alpha-linoleic acid have an important function although our bodies are not able to produce them. They are referred to as essential fatty acids, which basically means that we need to source them from our diet, as our bodies cannot generate them ourselves.

Handy Hint: Refined rapeseed oil can be heated up and enhances the flavour of foods, because it is largely tasteless. The fine, nutty flavour of cold pressed rapeseed oil is very tasty and lends itself perfectly to salad dressings, dips and sauces.

Alpha-linoleic acid has been in the news for years; not only because of its LDL lowering effects, but also because of it lowers triglycerides while at the same time increasing HDL levels.

While rapeseed oil has a valuable arrangement of fatty acids, it also has plenty of fat-soluble Vitamin E and A that protect polyunsaturated fatty acids from oxidising. We reached a point, particularly after the 1970s when potentially damaging rapeseed components have been genetically engineered and eliminated so that we have produced an ideal composition of fatty acids.

Red Rice

We all know that rice should form part of a healthy diet, and that this is the case in many Asian countries. What we have not so much realised is that rice is a cholesterol fighter. Red fermented rice also referred to as angkak or red-yeast rice is part of the staple diet in China.

At the start of the fermentation process, the rice is cultivated with the mold Monascus purpureus that gives it its bright red color. U.S. studies highlight its immense heart protective properties; at the same time, scientists have identified substances that have similar effects to those of the classic lipid-lowering agents.

The cholesterol lowering effects of ground rice capsules were tested in people over a period of eight weeks. The results showed that the total cholesterol value was reduced on average by 17 percent, the LDL value by even 22 percent. Although the HDL blood value remained constant, triglycerides were reduced by eleven percent. Red rice is generally available in Asian food shops.

Skillet Red Rice

This tasty and mild Spanish rice is the perfect complimentary side dish for any spicy Mexican or Spanish recipe!

Ingredients:	Notes:	Measurements
Vegetable oil		2 tablespoons
Long-grain rice	Raw	1 cup
Onion	Finely chopped	½ cup
Garlic clove	Minced	1
Salt		½ teaspoon
Cumin	Ground	½ teaspoon
Chilli Power	Pure/Hot	Pinch
Tomatoes	Large Peeled/Seeded/ Chopped	2
Chicken Broth		1 ½ cups
Peas	Fresh or frozen will work	1/3 cup

Directions:

1. Chop onion finely and set aside

2. Peel tomatoes

3. Remove seeds from tomatoes, chop and set aside

4. Add oil to a medium sized skillet and cook over a low to medium heat until the oil is hot

5. Pour rice into oil and cook over medium heat for 2 minutes stirring occasionally

6. Add chopped onion into the skillet and sauté onion for approximately 2-3 minutes

7. Add spices into skillets (Chili powder, cumin, salt and garlic)

8. Stir seasonings into rice thoroughly

9. Place tomatoes into skillet with other ingredients and cook for 2-3 minutes stirring occasionally

10. Pour chicken broth into the rice mixture

11. Turn the heat up to a medium-high setting and cover the skillet with a tight fitting lid

12. Allow mixture to come to a boil and then reduce heat to low

13. Leave rice to simmer for about 15 minutes

14. Remove lid and add fresh or frozen peas into the rice mixture

15. Stir all ingredients together thoroughly

16. Replace lid and allow rice to steam over a low heat for an additional 3-5 minutes

17. Turn off heat and remove skillet

18. Allow rice to sit for 5-10 minutes before serving

Safflower Oil

Safflower oil is plant-based cooking oil that is generated from the seed of the safflower. It has very few saturated and mono-unsaturated fatty acids and in addition to being high in Vitamin E, it has a high proportion of LDL-lowering as well as poly-unsaturated fatty acids. Safflower oil has the highest share of all plant-based fats, and is therefore available as low-fat cooking oil.

When you prepare delicious cholesterol reducing salad dressings, only use high-quality cold-pressed safflower oil or margarine that is high in safflower oil. As with all cold-pressed cooking oils, you should not use it to cook as it will start smoking at low temperatures.

If you need to cook at hot temperatures you should principally only use refined oils. They should be stored in dark, cool and closed environments, as they have a high proportion of unsaturated fatty acids and are susceptible to oxidation.

Salmon

Salmon is a typical representative of fatty sea fish. In contrast to other fatty meats, fat-rich fish is considered one of the healthy types of animal foods. Because of its high content in Omega-3, salmon is considered one of the real cholesterol friendly foods. Much research confirms its importance in providing one of the most important sources of Omega-3 fatty acids.

Regular consumption of salmon can improve the blood velocity. Arteries remain elastic, triglyceride and LDL-cholesterol levels are reduced and HDL values increase. Nutrition experts have suggested for a long time that we eat fish at least twice a week.

An extensive study of thousands of participants into the prevention of heart attacks showed that people who have already suffered one heart attack can greatly improve their chance of survival and reduce the risk of suffering a second attack by maintaining a diet rich in fish and fish oils.

Handy Hint: Obtain your fish from sustainable fisheries! The MSC label was invented some years ago to protect the seas from over-fishing. These MSC labeled products come from environmentally-friendly businesses.

Garden Patch Salmon Dinner

Serves 2

This delicious salmon recipe is awesome when served over potatoes or try it with your favorite rice or pasta as well for a tasty variation! You can add more tomatoes as well to increase the amount of gravy that the recipe yields if you like!

Ingredients:	Notes:	Measurements
Salmon fillets	2	Approximately ½ pound
Yukon Gold Potatoes	Large/Mashed	2
Plain Yogurt	Greek or Regular Varieties	¼ cup
Salt & Pepper		To Taste

Olive Oil		3 tablespoons
Basil	Fresh	¼ cup
Garlic Cloves	Minced	2
Sun Dried Tomatoes	Packed in Oil/Chopped (Optional)	1 Tablespoon
Snap Peas or Frozen Peas	Use one or the Other	½ Cup
Cherry Tomatoes	Cut in Half	½ Cup

Directions:

1. Defrost Salmon in microwave if frozen or allow it to sit out until thoroughly thawed.

2. Turn on the oven and allow it to preheat to a temperature of 350F

3. Peel and dice Yukon potatoes

4. Boil potatoes in a medium sized pot until soft

5. Remove potatoes from water and strain

6. Add yogurt to the potatoes along with salt and pepper

7. Mash potatoes and yogurt together

8. Pour olive oil into a large skillet

9. Turn on the heat to medium-high to heat the oil thoroughly

10. Place garlic, basil and sundried tomatoes into the hot oil and cook until the garlic begins to brown

11. Add peas to the pan and stir all ingredients together

12. Place the potatoes evenly into two separate casserole dishes

13. Place the peas and seasoning mixture onto the top of the potatoes and yogurt mixture

14. Place the tomatoes onto the top of each casserole dish

15. Place one salmon filet onto the top of each one

16. Brush the oil and seasoning mixture from the pan over the top of each dish and then place into the oven uncovered

17. Allow it to cook for approximately 25 minutes or until thoroughly heated

18. Serve each casserole dish individually.

Sesame Oil

Sesame seed presumably is one of the oldest vegetable oils in the world. The smaller seeds are used to produce lighter oil that is neutral in taste, and roasted seeds yield darker, nutty oil. It is rich in Vitamin E, and contains more than 80 percent of mono-and polyunsaturated fatty acids, half of which consist of linoleic acid,

What is more, sesame oil has a respectful amount of LDL cholesterol lowering phytosterols. Like all other high-quality oils, sesame oil should be kept cool and in the dark. Don't forget that the seeds themselves contain valuable oils as well. The small and aromatic seeds are a great addition to biscuits, rolls and muesli.

Handy Hint: If you want to ensure a varied and effective cholesterol lowering diet you may find it helpful to have small bottles of different types of oil in storage: cold-pressed flaxseed, rapeseed, safflower, sesame- and pumpkinseed oil for raw food meals and salads, as well as refined flax and sunflower oil for hot meals. Use small amounts of two different kinds daily.

Make use of the health benefits of sesame twice in one meal: create a hearty wok dish made up of freshly sliced vegetables fried in a little sesame oil, and just before serving add a few sesame seeds on top.

Shiitake Mushrooms

Mushrooms consist of about 90 percent water, they are low in calories and perfect for maintaining a healthy weight. In traditional Chinese medicine Shiitake has culinary as well as medicinal uses. This mushroom is used to strengthen your immune system, as well as for the prevention and treatment of bowel disease and infections.

If consumed regularly, the Shiitake mushroom that is native to East Asia can also prevent cardio-vascular problems. This tree mushroom can be considered vital to our health because it has unsaturated fatty acids as well as choline that can help lower your cholesterol levels.

Fresh and dried mushrooms are available in Asian food stores and well-supplied supermarkets. Dried specimens have to be soaked for some hours in advance before boiling or frying them, at which point they are a delicious addition to your diet. A daily portion of Shiitake mushrooms will turn them into cholesterol fighters. It is however easier to resort to the appropriate food supplements.

Miso Soup with Shiitake Mushrooms and Tofu

Serves 1

This healthy low cholesterol and sodium recipe is both nutritious and delicious; which makes this soup is the perfect dinner for a cold winter's night!

Ingredients:	Note:	Measurements
Water		½ pint
Shitake Mushrooms		2
Scallion		1
Miso		1 Tablespoon
Tofu	Diced	1 Ounce

Directions:

1. Place Mushrooms onto cutting board and cut into thin slices

2. Place Scallion on cutting board and cut the top green section into small diced bits

3. Place scallion in small dish to use as a garnish

4. Place water into a medium sized sauce pan and turn the heat to a medium-high setting

5. Allow water to come to boil and then add sliced mushrooms and miso

6. Reduce heat to low and allow ingredients to cook for 5 minutes

7. Pour from saucepan into a casserole dish

8. Place tofu onto the top of the cooked mixture

9. Place scallions over the top for garnish

10. For best taste serve right away

Soya

As with all plant foods, soybeans are cholesterol-free. This legume is largely consumed in Asia and hailed as a miracle bean. Many vegetarians regard it as a good source of protein. It contains soy lecithin that inhibits the absorption of cholesterol; and it stimulates the production of bile and HDL transport. Moreover, it is high in fiber, which has a positive impact on cholesterol levels. Protein does not usually have any effect on cholesterol or triglyceride levels.

However, if plant-based proteins are consumed, the intake of saturated fatty acids found in animal proteins, are reduced. As a cholesterol sufferer, you will experience the reduction of cholesterol levels if you decide to replace animal proteins with soybean protein and add more soy protein to your diet.

One study even shows this reduction to be an incredible 25 percent. But to get the most from the effects of the soybean, you should eat about 0.9oz of soy protein every day, which can be achieved by making soy drinks, by replacing yoghurt with soy-based products and by making a point of eating tofu and soy-based meat a couple of times per week.

Sunflower Oil

As late as the 16th century sunflower arrived in the 'old world' via Spanish seamen, where it was largely used as an ornamental plant. The key ingredients in sunflower oil that make it an effective cholesterol killer are a high volume of linoleic acid as well as the fat-soluble vitamins A and E. Vitamin E (tocopherol) can protect fatty acids against the damaging effect of oxidation and provides a protective shield for these vital ingredients.

Sunflower oil contains a sufficient amount of Vitamin E and therefore should be kept at cool temperatures in a dark environment only for up to a period of twelve months. It supports the immune system and improves the body's natural repair mechanisms in the cells, as well as the oxygen supply to the tissues and blood velocity.

In addition, sunflower seeds as well as cold-pressed oils contain a large amount of phytosterols.

A little margarine product information:

Margarine: Fat spread has 80-90 percent fat content. Even small amounts of animal based fats, for example found in milk or beef tallow are permissible.

Handy Hint: Fats and oils should principally not be cooked at high temperatures as they will otherwise start smoking and have health-damaging consequences. The point at which oil starts smoking is dependent on the amount of unsaturated fatty acids that it contains.

Vegetable margarines: 97 percent needs to consist of plant-based fats, and the proportion of linoleic acid should not go below 15 percent. Vegetable margarine, based on sunflowers for example, has to be produced by using 97 percent of these oils.

Vegetable margarines, rich in linoleic acid: its share of linoleic acid has to be at least 30 percent. However, 'very rich in linoleic acid' means that margarine should contain over 50 percent of linoleic acid.

Low-fat margarine may only consist of vegetable fats and oils. Its content of polyunsaturated fatty acids is above 40 percent. Some margarine, those that claim to have lipid-lowering effects, need to have at least 50 percent of those fatty acids. In terms of calorie values, butter and margarine are the same.

Some margarine may be referred to as 'half-fat margarine' which simply means it contains half the fat of the equivalent full-fat version. Typically you cannot use it for cooking, frying or baking.

There is also what is called a 'half-fat diet margarine' that could be considered the classical 'half-fat margarine' with phytosterols and can only be used as a spread, particularly for people with high blood lipid values. If you want to experience the full benefit of these special margarines, you should consume a daily amount of 1/4 cup

Vitamin E

Vitamin E is described as a group of chemicals with similar structural bonds, also referred to as tocopherols. Each of tycopherol's representatives have different biological activities, and that's why we need to consider that the effectiveness varies depending on their type, and that the daily recommended amount is counted in international units (I.U.). Nutrition experts would vary the recommended daily intake by age and sex between 18 to 23 I.U.; however, to achieve the desired cholesterol lowering effect of Vitamin E you should take 200 I.U. per day.

Vitamin E is not only effective in combating free radicals and inhibiting oxidation, it also acts on high levels of cholesterol and especially LDL levels: this alone makes Vitamin E an effective cholesterol fighter. Even better are the results when garlic, lecithin and the fat-soluble Vitamin E are combined. These cholesterol fighters are particularly effective in this combination.

In addition, you should also remember the benefits of dietary fiber and phytosterols. You can be assured that your blood lipid levels stand a high chance of returning to normal and avoid taking lipid lowering drugs.

Tocopherol is also used as an additive in the food industry. It acts by protecting fats, vitamins and natural coloring agents from damage from oxygen exposure, and is even classed among the organic foods.

Handy Hint: Preparing hearty, cholesterol reducing meals need not be complicated or time-consuming. Take one portion of spinach with garlic, and add one boiled egg and whole wheat bread with phytosterol margarine; potatoes with melted phytosterol margarine and add scrambled egg with tomato and onion salad and garlic. These are simple and effective meals that contain Vitamin E, lecithin, garlic, dietary fiber and phytosterols and that ensure that your blood lipids return to normal.

Walnuts

The Greeks believed that the walnut tree contained the wisdom of gods, and its nuts pass it to mankind. It was not so long ago that this 'celtic nut' was classified as "nut fruit" whereas before they were classed as "stone fruit".

Walnuts are singled out by their high content in several unsaturated fatty acids, one of which is the alpha-linolenic acid. The latter belongs to the incredibly valuable and essential Omega-3 fatty acids. In fact, the high Omega-3 content is responsible for the healthy effect of walnuts.

Studies conducted so far show that consuming walnuts lowers cholesterol levels and improves the elasticity of arteries.

Handy Hint: Walnuts can supplement your cereal breakfast, as well as any raw foods and salads. They can turn fruit salads and yoghurt or quark dishes into cholesterol friendly desserts. Studies show that despite their high energy content, consuming nuts or seeds daily basis does not increase your body weight. Quite the contrary: a handful of nuts every day can lead to weight reduction, which may be explained by the change in fat and energy metabolism.

Cranberry Relish with Apples and Walnuts

Serves 6

This delicious cranberry relish is the perfect side dish for a holiday celebration and will sure to become a family tradition!

Ingredients:	Note:	Measurements
Cranberries	Raw	8 ounces
Apples	Chopped	½ cup
Walnuts	Chopped	1 ½ cup
Sugar		2 Cups

Directions:

1. Cut the walnuts into small pieces

2. Place cranberries into the blender

3. Pour water into the blender until the surface of the cranberries are covered

4. Turn on the blender on a low setting until cranberries are thoroughly chopped

5. Drain water from cranberries

6. Place chopped cranberries into a bowl or casserole dish

7. Chop apples into small bite sized pieces

8. Place apples and walnuts in with the cranberries

9. Stir all ingredients together

10. Add sugar if you prefer and then mix everything together thoroughly

11. Allow the relish to sit in the refrigerator overnight before serving

Tips & Suggestions

- You can add sugar to taste if you want the relish to be sweeter

Try adding diced orange or apples to the relish for a tasty treat!

Connect With Lisa!

facebook.com/LisaLeesPage

Made in United States
North Haven, CT
27 April 2022

18669851R00055